AmericanGirl Library®

a smart girl's guide to boys

surviving crushes, staying true to yourself & other ♥ stuff

by Nancy Holyoke
illustrated by Bonnie Timmons

American Girl®

SCHOLASTIC INC.
New York Toronto London Auckland Sydney
Mexico City New Delhi Hong Kong Buenos Aires

ISBN 0-439-37565-7

12 11 10 9 8 7 6 5 4 3 2 3 4 5 6 7/0

Printed in the U.S.A. 24

First Scholastic printing, March 2002

Visit our Web site: americangirl.com

Editorial Development: Michelle Watkins, Judy Woodburn
Art Direction: Kym Abrams
Design: Jenny El-Shamy
Book Production: Kendra Pulvermacher, Janette Sowinski

Dear Reader,

Boys. You've grown up with them. They've been teammates and classmates, neighbors and pals. But most of the time, you and your friends sailed right on by the boys. They did their stuff. You did yours.

Now all that's changing. Kids are getting **crushes.** Girls are calling boys on the phone. Boys are hanging out with girls at the bus stop. Your friends are talking about who likes who. Boys may make you nervous and excited—but they may confuse you, too.

Boys are **different** from girls in lots of ways. Their brains are different, chemically and physically. Boys have different hormones, which make for different emotions. Plus, boys and girls are taught to act differently from the time they're babies. So if you've been thinking that talking to a boy is different from talking to a girl—guess what? You're right.

Of course you've got **questions.** What do you say to a boy? How can you tell if one likes you? How do you tell a boy you like him? What if your friend likes boys and you don't? What about boy-girl parties? Dances? And what, oh what, about r-e-j-e-c-t-i-o-n?

This book is a guide for all these things. It includes letters and **advice** from girls like you, as well as tips, quizzes, and even advice from boys themselves. You want to feel good and be yourself with boys, whether you've got a crush or not. You want to be part of the fun without losing your pride or your brain or your heart. We hope this book will make it easier for you to do that.

Your friends at American Girl

contents

Brave New World

Crushes 8

A typical day 10

Hormones 12

Staying normal 13

Who Likes Who

"Liking" a boy 18

Getting to know a boy 19

Conversation starters 20

What boys want 21

Should you tell him you like him? 24

What's he thinking? 25

How to tell him you like him 28

Mistake o' the day 31

Getting no for an answer 32

Unattainable boys 34

Turning down a boy 35

Pop quiz: Are you feeling rushed? 37

Pop quiz: Are you boy crazy? 39

So, what are the rules? 41

Talking to parents 43

Life in the Fishbowl

Boys & friends 47
Changing interests 48
Rx for an ailing friendship 50
Secrets 52
How to keep a secret 56
Competition & jealousy 57
Boy buds 60
Boys vs. buds 64
Boys online 68
Parties & dances 70
Popularity 72
Teasing & harassment 76
Pop quiz: Peer pressure 80

Going Together

Twosomes 84
Pop quiz: Why pair off? 85
Things to do when you go out 86
Touching 88
Kissing basics 91
Trouble-starters 92
Solving problems 94
Problem boyfriends 96
Pop quiz: Problem girlfriends 98
Pop quiz: Time to break up? 101
How to break up 103
Getting dumped 105

Taking Care of You

Pop quiz: How are you doing? 108
Happy ever after? 112

Brave New World

crushes

I am crush crazy about this boy. He's cute and he's funny. He has red hair and he wears baggy shorts. He is very cute. He's COOL. And he knows a lot of stuff. He's so cute.

Mad about him

Lots of kids—boys and girls alike—have crushes from the time they go off to preschool. But as you reach puberty, those crushes may get bigger. Tiny crushes, which in first grade took up a corner of your brain, can become

huge, humongous, gigantic

crushes that make you look out the window for hours instead of studying for your math test.

You might have a crush on a rock star. You might have a crush on a teacher or your cousin or your friend's big brother. You might have a crush on a boy at school who doesn't even know your name.

These kinds of crushes can make you feel **wonderful** because . . .

you have **excited,** happy feelings,

you have wonderful **daydreams,**

you can feel romantic about someone **without the risk** that that person might hurt your feelings **(it's safe),**

and you will never have to face the fact that your crush is **not perfect.**

Crushes are also a natural part of growing up. A crush lets you try on all kinds of new feelings, sort of like going into a store and trying on all kinds of clothes without having to buy them. You can learn a lot. You experience romantic feelings. You consider what you like in other people. You learn how to deal with frustration when you can't get what you want. All of this helps you get ready for the day you get into a real relationship with someone.

Of course, you may also develop a crush on a boy you actually know. Kids around you may be getting crushes, too. Some may even be speaking up and saying so. This can make life at school **very** different.

a typical day

Suddenly kids are talking about who likes who. School is a more gossipy, less private place. There's more intrigue—and more nervousness, too.

8:45 A.M.
Lindsey tells Caitlin she likes Brett. 

10:05 A.M.
Caitlin tells Brett that Lindsey likes him. Brett says, "Uh, ur, well, Lindsey's O.K."

10:36 A.M.
Maria writes her favorite rock star's name on her notebook cover for the 348th time.

11:05 A.M.
Caitlin tells ten of her closest friends (including Lindsey) that Lindsey and Brett are now going together.

11:47 A.M.
Joaquin sits near Ashley at lunch. What does it mean? Ashley has no idea.

11:50 A.M.
Lindsey says hi to Brett in the cafeteria. Brett says hi back. They both sit with their friends.

12:01 P.M.
Max and Megan ignore each other when they dump their trays. They are neighbors and good friends, but they never let on at school because they'd be teased.

1:30–1:45 P.M.

Lindsey writes a note to Brett and folds it up till it's the size of a wad of chewing gum. She gives it to Caitlin to deliver.

2:10 P.M.

Angela and Jing and Clementine have a good time in gym getting teased by David and DeShay and Reese.

3:00–3:30 P.M.

Caitlin gives Lindsey's note to Brett. She thinks he looks cute when he's embarrassed. On the bus, Caitlin makes a list of all the boys she's gone with this year. It looks like this:

1. Brett (2 weeks)
2. Khalid (1 week)
3. Joaquin (2 days)
4. David (3 1/2 hours)
5. Maggie's older brother, Jonathan (in her dreams)

There were others first semester, but she lost count. She thinks maybe she'd like to go with Brett again after he and Lindsey break up. She figures her friend and her new crush will last about 2 weeks.

Maybe 1.

hormones

What's caused all this drama? For one thing: hormones.

Hormones are chemicals in the body. During puberty, a girl's hormones help her body develop into a woman's body, and a boy's hormones help his body develop into a man's body. Hormones cause lots of emotional changes. They also change the way girls and boys look at one another.

We all know that puberty can start in one kid at nine and the next kid at 13. But, in general, hormones start working in girls a little sooner than they do in boys. This means that many girls may be taller and more physically mature than most boys their age up until high school. For the same reason, girls are often ready to be interested in boys earlier than boys are ready to be interested in them. That difference can lead to **confusion and disappointment** for girls.

staying normal

I don't have any problem being myself around girls, but sometimes when boys are around, I can't seem to be me. I just act weird.

Breeanna

A lot of girls find it hard to act normal. The simplest thing—like passing an assignment to the boy in the next desk—may send clouds of questions rolling through your mind.

So what's **weird?** For instance:

You act too cool

Louis is cute, Zach is awesome, and Ian is cool. You have to walk past them all on the way to your locker. You put a big smile on your face, pretend you're a movie star, and hope they buy the act.

Weird-O-Meter Rating: 

Most of us put up a front when we're nervous. Acting relaxed is the next best thing to feeling that way. It helps a person stay in control. But the goal is to look like yourself, not to look like someone else. So don't overdo the cool. Get the movie star out of your head, and picture yourself the way you were coming off the soccer field after the last winning game.

You talk too much

Ahmad is standing next to you in line. Suddenly you hear yourself jabbering away as if your mouth weren't connected to your brain.

Weird-O-Meter Rating: 

Slow down. It will give you time to think before you speak. Don't run your words together. Take a breath between sentences. Ask questions. Conversations involve both people talking, after all. And while he's looking for words, you'll have more time to get a grip on your own.

You laugh like a hyena

Manuel cracks a joke. You go heeheeheeheehee-heeheeheeheeheeheeheeheeheeheeheeheehee-heeheeheeheeheeheeheeheeheeheeheeheehee-heeheeheeheehee—and can't stop until the teacher walks up and raps on your desk.

Weird-O-Meter Rating 

Giggling too much makes you look hysterical. You're just not good company if you're out of control. So close your mouth, freeze your chest, and hold your breath for a moment. Glance away. Do something with your hands—grab a pencil, fool with the straps of your backpack. Concentrate on pulling yourself together, and don't relax till you do.

You pretend you're invisible

C.J. and Matt are so cute! They're talking to your best friend during a break in gym. You'd like to join them, but what if you say the wrong thing? You stay where you are and count bricks in the wall.

Weird-O-Meter Rating: 

Try not to avoid boys. It will only make your nerves worse. Remind yourself that it's natural for girls and boys to be fluttery around one another at this age. The way to learn to talk to boys is to talk to boys. Practice makes perfect. Or, at least, with a little practice, talking to boys won't be such a big deal.

Who Likes Who?

"liking" a boy

I have a group of really great friends who are each unique and creative in their own way. Some of them happen to be boys. There's this one kid I've known since the third grade, but now that we're getting older, I'm starting to like him differently (if you know what I mean).

Meg

Chances are that, for years, you've had certain ideas about the boys around you.

The boys you've always liked will probably be the same kind of boys you end up "liking." In fact, some girls who have had boy buddies for years may find that their feelings for them are beginning to change. Is that boy you have fun talking to a "friend" or a "boyfriend"? All of a sudden, you may not be quite sure.

getting to know a boy

I would really like to have a boy for a friend.
Elizabeth

You may find yourself looking at a certain boy and wondering how you can get to know him better.

For starters, be friendly. Run a smile up the flagpole. Say hi in the hall. If you're in the same study group, ask what he thinks of the new gym teacher or compliment him on his orange socks. Trade tips if you sit behind him in computer class. Show you're interested.

Look for common interests, too.

do you play the sax?

read science fiction?

snowboard?

kick a mean hacky sack?

Maybe he does, too. Ask some questions, and see what you share.

For that matter, if you're looking for a boy to be friends with, your own activities are a great place to start. Doing something fun together is the best way of getting to know anybody—girl or boy. It's just a whole lot easier to feel relaxed with a person if you're both swept up in shooting baskets or playing Ping-Pong or practicing your lines for the class play—not just staring at each other trying to think of what to say.

Conversation starters

Things to say when you're staring at a boy trying to think of what to say:

Ask about his **activities.** It's friendly and gets him talking.

Schoolwork: a subject about which there is always something to say.

Jokes get a smile and invite a comeback. And making fun of yourself shows you're relaxed and approachable.

It can be fun to rehash the great parts from a **movie** or **TV show.**

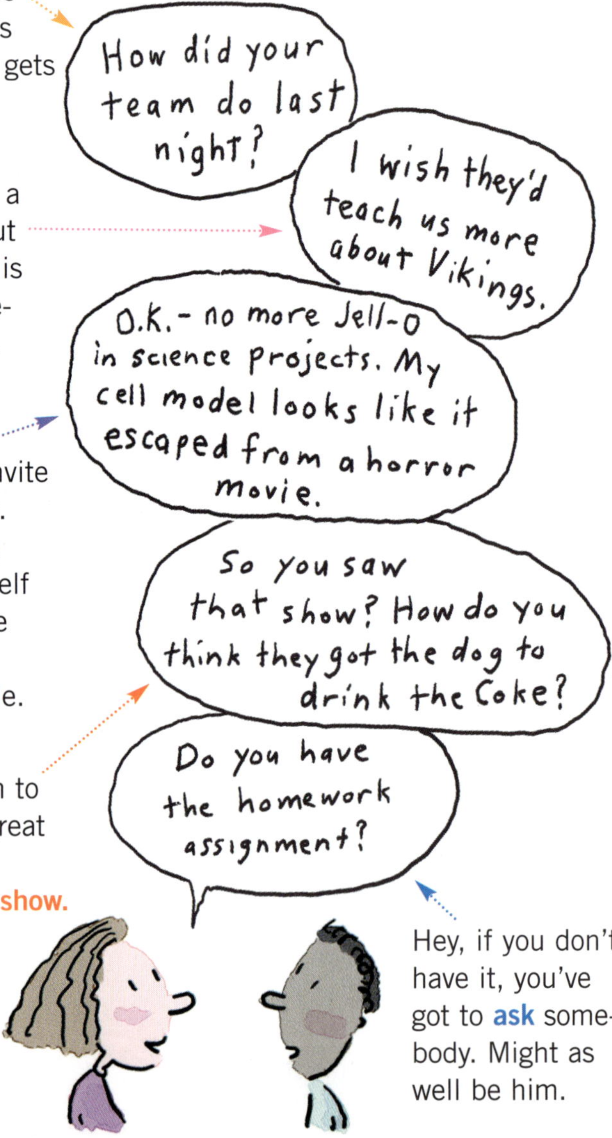

Hey, if you don't have it, you've got to **ask** somebody. Might as well be him.

what boys want

The guy I like is not popular or cute, but the thing is, he's nice. And he's fun. He's also cool. I'm not sure he likes me. I have not tried to change myself, but I wonder if I should.
Crush crazy

You'll know you have a crush on a boy if being near him feels a little like the flu.

How do you get him to notice you? Well, you could:

Take up skydiving.

Put a photo of yourself
in his ham sandwich.

Flirt till you drop.

Dress like a rock star.

Lie down in front of him in the hallway.

But, as any boy would tell you, it shouldn't require that much effort. What do boys look for in a girl? Glad you asked:

A good personality and a good sense of humor. Someone who is nice and can make me laugh.

Andrew, age 12

A girl who's willing to go places, who's not scared to talk to me.

Grant, age 13

Someone who is attractive, funny, and nice. She has to not drag me into malls.

Joey, age 13

Someone who's willing to be there for me when I'm in need.

James, age 12

Smart, cute, fun to be around. Happy and talented.

Aaron, age 13

Someone who likes me for me, and doesn't care what I look like.

Adam, age 13

I appreciate it when girls are themselves, when they don't act all phony and stuff.

Connor, age 12

So before you buy a bucket of makeup or change your name or dump old friends for new, hoping to attract that special boy, ask yourself this: "Is this going to make me happier to be me?"

Unless the answer is **yes,** don't do it.

should you tell him you like him?

I really, really, really like this boy in my class, but I'm afraid to tell him that I like him. I'm afraid he'll say something like "Gross!" or tell his friends and have everyone laughing at me.

Boy crazy in Illinois

For some girls, having a crush is a private thing. They're not ready to go public with how they feel.

Other girls would like the boy to know, if they weren't afraid of one little thing:

Everybody worries about it, boys and girls both. Nobody wants to get hurt. Nobody wants to be embarrassed. Nobody wants to find out that the person she's had a crush on doesn't feel the same way about her. It's always a gamble, letting a boy know you like him. But you can cut your risk a lot if you take some time to read a boy's signs before you speak up.

what's he thinking?

Most boys will give some pretty obvious signals about how they feel by the way they behave.

Funny looks

I really like this one guy. Just about every time he sees me, he gives me this long (not mean) stare. Is this good or bad?

Puzzled

Staring could be good. It could also mean your shirt tag is hanging out. Find an excuse to talk to him: make a remark about your classwork or the Hawaiian Surprise pizza in the lunchroom. See what happens. Maybe he'll grunt and turn away. Maybe he'll grin and blush and tell you what he did with his pizza after he scraped off the pineapple. Either way, you'll have your answer.

Wise guy

There's this boy that I like, and I think he likes me, but I'm not sure. For example: At recess he says, "Hi, Psycho." But he also unfreezes me when we play freeze tag with our friends. What should I think?

Not sure about love

Boys express affection for their friends by kidding around. They often do the same thing with a girl they like. A boy who teases you in a fun way could indeed have a crush on you. If he says "Hi, Psycho" and makes a big point of unfreezing you at tag? It's a good bet.

Loner

I like a boy I know. My brother said that the boy said he wants to be single, live in a trailer park, and be a sports announcer. I want to go out with him, but he's afraid to go out with anyone. Should I ask him out or keep my feelings a secret?

Single and Lonely

This boy may indeed not want to have anything to do with girls—now or ever. Or he may just talk that way because he doesn't want to get hurt by one. Try to get to know him. Be friendly. Talk. But go slow. Don't put pressure on him by demanding a lot of his time or attention. And don't talk about "liking" each other or being "girlfriend and boyfriend" or "going out." He's not ready for romance now, but if he learns he can trust you, that might change. If it doesn't, you'll still have a friend.

Mixed message

I have a boy problem, and I don't know what to do. He's really cute, nice, and unbelievably sweet. Oh, and he's really funny. He doesn't like me like I like him, but he said we should be really good friends. That's O.K. Just one problem. He doesn't talk to me or do anything with me, and sometimes he avoids me.

Boy Prob

When your heart's saying yes, yes, yes, it can be hard to see that a boy's trying to say no, no, no. You have to look at his actions, not just his words. This boy wants to be nice, friendly, and respectful. But he doesn't want to be your boyfriend, and by the sound of it, he doesn't want to be "really good friends," either. If you force yourself on him, he'll avoid you. If you want to be friends at all, back off.

Shy guy

My friends and I have a crush on this one boy. We don't know who he likes, but he knows who likes him. He's very shy and won't admit who he likes. We've asked him many times, and we've told him we like him. What should we do?

Clueless

It could be that this boy is shy. It could be that his hormones haven't really kicked in yet, and he feels about girls the way you felt about boys two years ago: indifferent. In either case, he's not ready to have a romantic relationship with you or your friends. To question him again and again will only embarrass him. For now, cross him off your list.

how to tell him you like him

You've been watching for signs. You think he might like you. You're ready to tell him you like him. How do you do it?

Well, some girls will write a letter. The problem is that once you put your words down on that paper, you can't be sure where they'll end up. Will his eyes be the only eyes that see them? Maybe.

But ~~maybe~~ probably not.

Nine out of ten middle-schoolers will get a friend to tell him. This has its advantages. If he says he doesn't like you, you don't have to melt into a puddle of embarrassment right at his feet. On the other hand, it's peculiar when you think about it. If you like a guy, shouldn't you be able to **talk to him** yourself?

Ten better ways to tell him you like him:

1. Sit behind him on the bus. Strike up a conversation. If you both have a good time, sit in the same spot tomorrow.

2. Offer him that extra ticket you have to the concert.

3. Put your towel next to his at the pool.

4. Go to one of his games, or ask if he'd like to come to one of yours.

5. Ask him to dance at the school dance.

6. Call him on the phone, and ask if he and his friends would like to go with you and your friends to the school play.

7 → Ask him and his friends to join you and your friends in a game of basketball at recess.

8 → Tell him how much you liked that report he did on dust mites. Ask if he wants to work on the next project together.

9 → Make plans with your friends to go to Dairy Queen after school. Tell him, "You and your friends could meet us there if you want."

10 → Spot him at the school carnival? Say, "I challenge you to the rubber-duck ringtoss. Best two out of three. Loser buys pizza."

But where, you may ask, are the words "I like you"?

Nowhere.

You don't need a big declaration to let a boy know how you feel. It's going to be perfectly clear that you like him because you're being so friendly. If he's interested, he'll take you up on your invitations. If he's not, he won't. But it will be a whole lot easier on your feelings to hear "No, I can't go to DQ" than "No, I don't like you."

Mistake o' the Day

An overenthusiastic girl can turn off a boy. Play it smart and avoid these classic mistakes.

Monday

Don't follow him around all the time. Give the guy some air.

Tuesday

You're in charge of your feelings, but you're not in charge of his. You can't just order the boy to like you.

Wednesday

Snubbing people to impress a boy makes an impression, all right—but not the one you want.

Thursday

Saying bad things about other girls to make yourself look good makes you look bad.

Friday

Don't cry and plead. He'll resent the pressure it puts on him. And you simply don't want to look that desperate.

getting no for an answer

If you get no from a boy? It hurts. A lot. There's no question about it. And it can be humiliating, too—especially if you get the news in the hallway in front of an audience of his friends and yours. You're going to feel like crawling off and hiding in your pencil box.

What you need to **do,** though, is:

- Act as if it's **no big deal.**
- Smile and say, "Oh, well. **That's O.K.**"
- Get **busy** with something else: schoolwork, talking to a friend, eating lunch. Diving into some activity will take your mind off your feelings and help hide your hurt.
- If you feel like crying, find a **private place** where you can do it without the whole world watching.
- Crack a **joke.** It's a way of telling other people you're not going to collapse just because of one guy—and a way of telling yourself that, too.

What you **don't** want to do is:

- Try to **persuade** him to change his mind.
- Get **mad,** write nasty letters or e-mails, and treat him like an enemy.
- Get your **friends** involved. You want to talk to them, sure. But you don't want them running around carrying messages from this person to that, blowing things up into a major drama that the school will be talking about all week.
- Let people drag you into big **discussions** about how miserable you must feel. It will make you more miserable yet.
- **Ask** this boy next week if he's changed his mind.

Unattainable boys

Maybe he's a movie star. Maybe he's the black belt at karate who's five years older. Maybe he's a boy at school who has no interest in you. Whatever the situation, if you have feelings for a guy that aren't—or can't be—returned, it can be hard. When a boy's a lost cause, how do you get him out of your system?

Keep **busy.** Call friends. Make plans. Don't give yourself the chance to mope around the house.

You may have things that **remind you** of the boy—letters, pictures, the eraser nub he lent you in the library last year. Be your own best friend and remind yourself that no good can come from brooding over these relics. Give them one last sigh, then pitch them.

Make it a point to **get to know** some other boys. You may think that you will never like them the way you do Mr. Unattainable, and that may be true. But their friendship will distract you from your sadness and do you good.

turning down a boy

There's this boy at school, and he's really weird. Nobody really likes him. He makes these weird snorting noises. I always have to sit next to him. Today he asked me out. I don't want to hurt his feelings. What do I do?

SCARED TO SAY NO!

Of course, there are going to be times that you want to turn [illegible]

[illegible] sn't easy to do. But [illegible] ip that makes you [illegible] nerve to speak up for [illegible] it right.

[illegible] boy's invitation the way [illegible] him your attention [illegible] busy after school."

[illegible] ry. You're a nice guy, [illegible] better than "Uh, I don't [illegible] ow, maybe. Sorry." You [illegible] say you want to be friends [illegible]

You owe a boy respect—you don't owe him a yes. If a boy keeps hanging around when you wish he wouldn't, talk to him with stronger language: "I've said no, and you should accept that. You are embarrassing me and bullying me. I don't like it. You have to stop."

- **Keep the business as private as you can.** Don't blast the news all over school or let your friends do so, either.

- don't don't don't don't
don't
don't don't
don't don't
don't don't don't

don't make fun of this boy with your friends.

And if the boy is really, *really* geeky and weird and ugly and unpopular and embarrassing, and you can't even begin to believe that he would talk to you, and you never, ever in this lifetime would have anything to do with him, and you want to be sure everybody this side of the planet Neptune knows that . . .

Be as nice and respectful as you would be to anyone else. Every kid has feelings—feelings just like yours—whether he's "weird and embarrassing" or not. Don't forget it. Treat this boy the way you'd want to be treated yourself. He's put himself on the line by telling you he likes you. Talking him down in **any** way is a rotten thing to do.

are you feeling rushed?

Could this be you? Yes or no?

1. Your friend is meeting a boy at the mall. He's bringing another boy, who's supposed to be for you. You feel sick to your stomach.

2. A boy tells you he likes you. You don't dislike him, but you don't like him, either—at least not like *that.* You're so uncomfortable, you could die.

3. Your friends are talking about who likes who. You're bored out of your mind. Have aliens hidden in their lockers and sucked out their brains? It all seems so silly!

4. You've had a crush or two. But when you think about getting teased, getting dumped, and having a boy touch you, you think: *Boys just aren't worth it.*

answers

Ready

If you answered mostly **no,** you feel ready for boys. You're comfortable with the idea of new kinds of relationships and don't feel threatened by the dramas and gossip of the world of who likes who. **That's fine.**

Not ready

If you answered mostly **yes,** you don't feel ready. **That's O.K., too.** People are different. There isn't a reason in the world to get pulled into situations that make you uncomfortable. There isn't a reason in the world to rush into relationships with boys, either. There are still going to be boys around a few years from now, when you're ready for them. If your gut tells you to stay on the sidelines, stay on the sidelines.

are you boy crazy?

POP QUIZ

What sounds most like you? Circle your answer.

1. Dylan sits down at the table behind you.
   a. You feel fluttery inside but keep talking with your friends.
   b. You say, "Oh, my gosh. There he goes!" and keep talking with your friends.
   c. You squeal and laugh till Dylan overhears you and moves to another table. Your friends are more embarrassed than you are.

2. You're at the pool with your friends when Xavier walks in.
   a. You say hi when he swims past your water-basketball game.
   b. You watch him out of the corner of your eye. When he goes to the snack bar, you snag a friend and follow.
   c. Friends? What friends? You're going to stick to this guy like fresh gum. (Why else would you be at the pool to begin with?)

3. There's a big science test tomorrow.
   a. You study for it.
   b. You call a friend and gossip for a half hour about your crush. Then you study for the test.
   c. You call Mike twice, Muneeb three times, and Joel four. You glance at your science, then call a friend to tell her what the boys said.

4. You've always wanted to learn to water ski. Now the youth group's at the lake and you have your chance. James is there, too.
   a. You head straight for the dock to learn to water ski.
   b. You spend an hour trying to talk James into getting wet.
   c. You stay on the shore. If James isn't skiing, you aren't, either.

5. You make a list of the guys you like.
   a. It has one or two names.
   b. It has three or four names.
   c. You're still writing.

answers

Self-reliant

If you answered mostly **a**'s, you've got things to do, places to go, friends to see. If a boy turns up along the way, that's O.K. But if not, that's O.K., too. You've got an independent spirit and a healthy self-respect. Other people will like you for it. Better yet, you'll like yourself.

Wishful

If you answered mostly **b**'s, you're willing to make some compromises for a boy. But spend your time running after him? You're not that far gone yet.

Carried away

If you answered mostly **c**'s, you're overboard. It makes you seem silly. Let's be honest. A boy wants a girl with a life of her own—not a girl with a head so full of crushes that there's no room for anything else. And when you stop to think about it, isn't that what you want for yourself, too?

Happiness doesn't come from getting the right boy to call. It comes from **feeling good** about what you can do and working toward things you care about. So chill out on the boys. Pay attention to you. If you don't think you're worth it, why should anyone else?

so, what are the rules?

Q: Is it O.K. for a girl to call a boy?

A: Sure. Just use the same phone manners you use with everybody else.

No calls after nine o'clock at night. No prank calls. No hanging up before the person gets to the phone. No goofy group calls at midnight from slumber parties.

And watch the time. Don't talk forever. Tying up your phone and his for hours on end is a major annoyance to both families. Don't keep calling back, either. If you're getting the homework assignment or arranging what time to meet after soccer, you can call again. But if you want to go over the day's gossip for the third time? 'Fraid not.

Q: Is it O.K. for a girl to like an older boy?

A: Lots of girls get crushes on older boys. Flirting with a friend's older brother or the lifeguard at the pool is as traditional as sun in August. You both know it's a game. You're out to have fun, and that's it. And that's fine.

But is it O.K. to have an actual romantic relationship with a guy that old? No. No way. It doesn't matter how nice he is. He's at an entirely different stage of growing up. He's far more experienced than you are. He's far stronger physically. It cannot be an equal relationship or anything close to one. A girl who accepts romantic advances from a much older boy is in real danger of being taken advantage of. Don't do it.

Q: At what age is it O.K. for a girl to have a boyfriend?

A: Your parents set the rules on this one. The answer will depend on their beliefs, on your age, and on what you mean by "boyfriend."

In lots of first romances, a boyfriend is the guy you talk to on the phone and hang out with at school in a big group of friends. If you're a little older, you and your girlfriends may go to dances or movies with a bunch of boys, knowing that some of you are sort of paired off. If you're older yet, you and a boy may pair off for real and go out on an actual date.

If you're, say, 12, your parents may be O.K. with the first kind of relationship but not O.K. with the last. They're also sure to have ideas about what kinds of physical touching are appropriate for a girl your age.

Some girls don't want to talk to their parents about crushes because they think their parents will disapprove. Others don't talk to their parents because they're afraid their parents will make fun of them. Certainly both things can happen. But you and they are going to need to talk about these issues in the coming years. Look for ways to start the conversation now.

Pick a time that's made for talking—when you're together in the car or folding laundry right before bedtime. Tell your mom or dad a thing or two about what's going on at school. Talk about how you're feeling. Ask your parents about their own first crush. It'll feel good to break the ice on this subject. It will also be that much easier to talk freely about boy issues once you've found some common ground.

Talking to parents

You want your parents to hear you when you've got something to say. So don't make these age-old mistakes:

Go slow. Try not to fly off the handle. You miss the chance to communicate a lot of good information if you go from Point A to Point Z in a single bound. For one thing, you need to be sure you and your parents are talking the same language. "Going out" may not mean the same thing to them as it does to you. Listen to them, as you expect them to listen to you. Talk it through.

If you hear yourself making **accusations,** pull back. Point to ways in which you've already proved you're responsible instead. Keep your voice reasonable. It will show how mature you are and keep them listening.

Shut down the conversation with comments like this, and your parents will never understand your point of view. How could they if you give up on explaining? Hang in there. Take a deep breath. Take another one. Be patient.

The last thing that will bring your parents to your way of seeing things is a **threat.** If you feel you've run out of self-control, say, "I need to cool down for a bit," and go to your room. Pound your pillow if you need to. Then get out some paper and start planning what you'll say when you come back out.

Silence can be better than saying something you'll regret. But it's a temporary fix, a Band-Aid on a raw spot. Make a pact with your mom and dad: however much you disagree, you'll always hear each other out. There's a lot of future stretching out ahead of you and your family. Keep talking. You'll be glad you did.

Life in the Fishbowl

Can he tell what I'm thinking?
A heart that can break.
Weak in the knees

girl

How does he see me?
A head full of what??
What's he feeling?

boy

boys & friends

One boy. One girl. It should be so simple! But it's **not.**

There are **your friends.** And **his friends.** Not to mention the rest of the school. Sit with a boy at lunch, and every kid in the state has heard about it by the time you get on the bus. It's like living in a fishbowl. **Everybody knows** what everybody else is doing—and has an opinion about it. Including, of course, your friends.

They may think the boy you like is just fine.
(They may even **like him themselves.)**

They may think he's a lower life-form
(and **tease** you till you wonder what you ever saw in him yourself).

What they probably won't do is keep quiet.

(talk
talk
talk
whisper
whisper
gossip
gossip)

One way or the other, the minute you get involved with a boy, your friends are going to be involved with that relationship, too.

changing interests

My best friend is angry because I like a boy. How can I like a boy without breaking our friendship and losing someone I trust?

Worried

I've been best friends with this girl for three years. Now we're in sixth grade. But she's changed. Now that she's got a boyfriend, it's as if I weren't even there. We used to do everything together.

Left Out

Different feelings about boys can cause trouble in the strongest of friendships. You and your friend may have shared sleepovers and secrets and Skittles since first grade, but if one of you gets interested in boys and the other doesn't, you're pulling in opposite directions. All of a sudden, the two of you are looking at each other and wondering where the magic went.

Sometimes the differences are so great that friends drift **a p a r t.** But that doesn't have to happen.

rx for an ailing friendship

If you have a boyfriend (or want one) and your friend doesn't:

- Don't ask the boy to come along every single time you go somewhere with your friend. **Save time** just for her.
- Don't **break a date** with your friend because the boy asked you to do something else. It's rude and annoying.
- Don't try to **convince her** that she should like boys, too. Telling a friend that she's slow or backward or uncool is not a smart move if you want to stay friends.
- Don't **talk** to your friend about this boy all the time. At best, it'll bore her. It may also make her feel jealous and left out.

If you **don't have** a boyfriend (and don't want one) but your friend does:

It's easy to get jealous. Remind yourself that friends and boyfriends are **different** things. Having a crush on a boy shouldn't make your friend like you any less.

Be **patient.** Some girls go boy crazy for a while, then calm down about the business. Give it time.

Try **sharing.** If you can accept the fact that your friend wants to spend time with a boy, and be cheerful when the three of you are together, you may find that having him in the picture isn't so bad after all. You may even have fun with him, too.

secrets

Friends who share an interest in boys can have problems, too, and some of the problems come from just **how much** they share.

For girls, talking is a big part of friendship. You and your friends may talk about your homework and the soccer game and what happened on your favorite TV show last night. But you probably also talk about friends, relationships, and feelings. Girls' conversations tend to be personal. Letting a friend into your private thoughts makes you feel closer to her, and feeling close feels good. Half the fun of having a crush is talking about it with your friends.

The problem is that your friends may enjoy talking and trading secrets as much as you do. And chances are that some of the secrets they're going to trade with others will be **yours.**

My best friend gave a note to the boy next to me. It said who I like. The note went around the classroom, and now everyone knows!!! I got so embarrassed, I almost cried. I can't believe what my best friend did.

Red-faced

I like someone in my school. If I tell my best friend, she'll tell the whole school. Then everyone will tease me and laugh at me.

Thea

I like this boy. We're friends. We talk a lot. But I made the mistake of telling my other friend about him, and she told him I wanted to kiss him. Gross! Now he won't talk to me.

Carrie

There's this girl. She can be nice. Then she can be a big pain. I'll tell her some things about my boyfriend, and she promises not to tell him. The next day, she goes and tells him everything I said.

Friendship problems

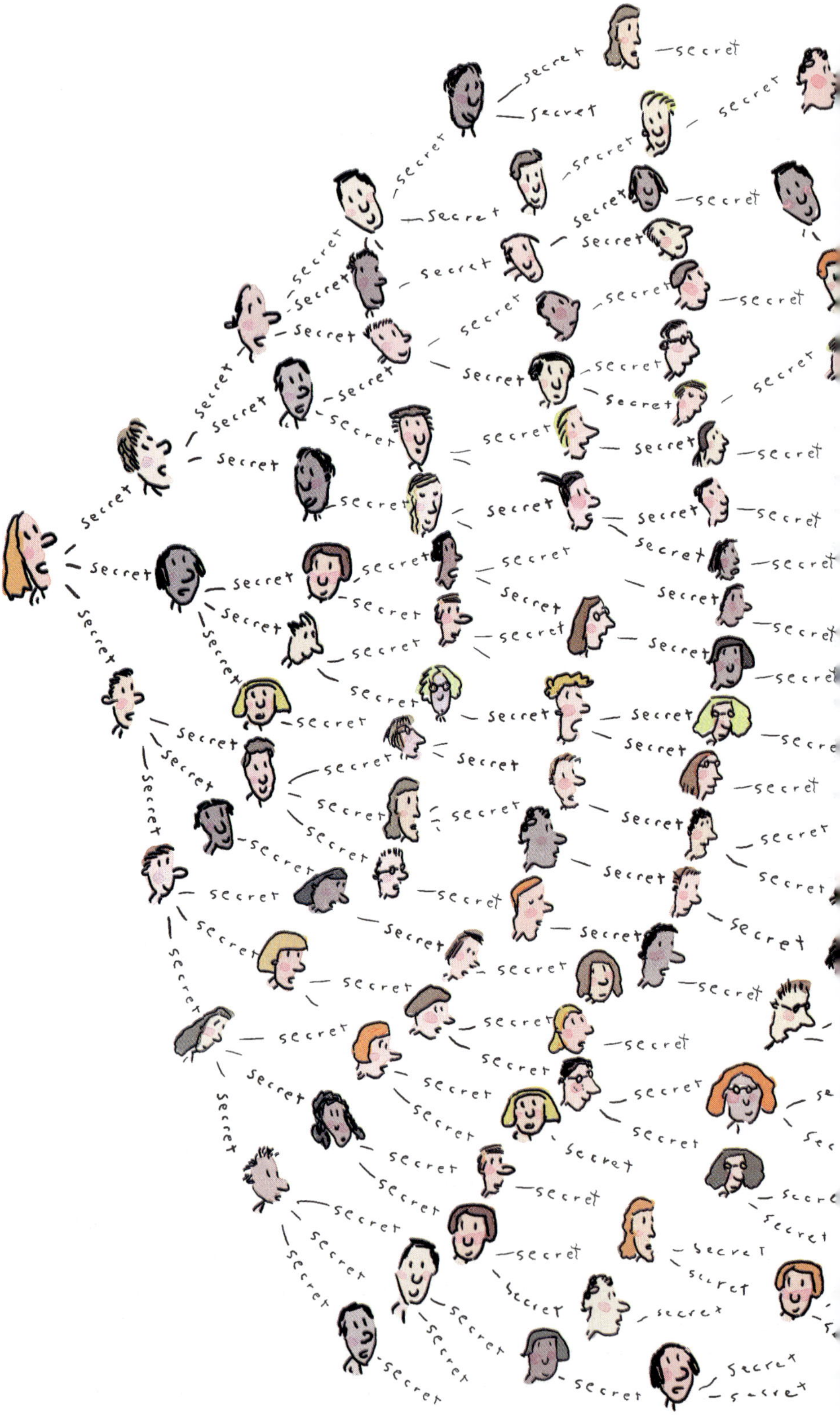

If you want 100% protection from situations like this:

★ **Don't tell anyone** to begin with. The only secrets you control are the ones you keep to yourself.

★ If you're going to burst if you don't talk, confide in a person who isn't part of your life at school—a member of your family, say, or a friend who lives on the other side of town, or your cousin in Buffalo.

★ If you still want to tell a friend so badly that you're willing to take the risk (that's R-I-S-K), then tell **one friend only,** and make it a good one. Think about it before you do it. Don't pick a girl you're trying to impress. Don't pick an on-again, off-again friend. Don't pick a girl who told your last secret, either. Some people just can't keep their lips zipped. If your best friend is one of them, you'll be better off recognizing that and confiding in someone else. You might also consider telling a friend who has confided a secret to you. If you kept hers, there's a better chance she'll keep yours.

How to keep a secret

A few thoughts to ward off temptation:

A lot of secrets are told on impulse. So make it a rule to **wait** two full minutes (check your watch) between the time it occurs to you to tell and the time you open your mouth.

The fun of telling a secret lasts a moment. The trouble it can cause may last for days, weeks—sometimes forever. Ask yourself, **"Is it worth it?"**

Remember the look on your **friend's face** the last time she found out that you told one of her secrets.

Remind yourself **how you felt** when somebody broke a promise and told a secret of yours.

What **kind of person** do you want to be? The kind you can trust or the kind you can't? Your pick.

competition & jealousy

(For that matter, it's very common for half the girls in the school to like the same boy.)

It's very common for friends to like the same boy.

Flirty friend

I have a big crush on this guy in my class. My best friend knows that I like him. Then one time I was spending the night at her house. She told me she had a crush on him, too. Now they sit next to each other in class, and she flirts with him.

Left-out

If you and this boy were a pair, your friend shouldn't do anything to break things up. But having a crush on the guy doesn't make him yours. There isn't really anything wrong with her talking to him in class. Joke with your friend about how jealous you are and hope for a new seating chart.

The wrong crush

My best friend has had a boyfriend for a year now, and I have a crush on him. I can't tell her or him or anybody!

Sarah

Having a crush on a friend's boyfriend comes pretty naturally. He may be the first boy you've talked to and spent time with. There isn't always a clear line between enjoying a boy's company and feeling romantic.

That said, remind yourself that this boy is off-limits. Be sure that nothing you do or say implies anything else. Turn your attention elsewhere. Chat up this boy's best buds. Dive into your guitar lessons—turn up the amp, sing some sad songs. Call another girlfriend. Tell yourself this crush is temporary. You're going to keep your eye on what matters most: your friendship.

Jealous[10]

I really like this boy in my class. One day at recess some of the girls (well, about ten) were talking about which boy they liked. ALL of them said the boy I like!!! Now I keep telling myself how bad the other girls are when deep inside I know they're not bad at all!

Miserable in Michigan

It's called jealousy. It can drive a girl crazy; it can drive friends apart. But you know what's eating you, and that's going to make this situation a whole lot easier to take. It's as you say: These girls aren't bad. They're just like you. And how weird would it be to blame them for that? Let your cool head guide you on this one. And don't forget to have some laughs with your friends about how many of you there are. Ten girls! A hockey team—plus subs!

Two-faced friend

A girl in my class likes the boy I like! She tries to get his attention every day. But when his back is turned—boom! She's my friend.

Jealous

You shouldn't get mad at this girl for being friendly to a boy she likes unless you think she'd be right to be mad at you for the same thing. But if she's ignoring you one minute and goes all gooey the next, that's not so great. Competing for the same guy should never mean turning your back on a friend.

Guilty feelings

I have loved a boy for over one year, but he's going out with one of my best friends. I heard that he was going to break up with her. I was happy at first, but then I thought about how sad my friend would be. But I'm still happy about it. Is that real, real bad?

happy but sad

It's not real, real bad, because you feel guilty about it: it shows you care about your friend and don't want to betray her. Act on that, and you'll be O.K. If the break-up happens, put her first. Listen to her talk. Give her time to get over him. At that point, you can look at this boy with a clear conscience.

boy buds

There's a boy at school and we're like best friends. I try to say this to my girlfriend. She just says, "That's what they all say." Now people at school are suggesting we go out. I wouldn't mind, except I don't want to ruin a great friendship.

torn

A year ago, being friends with a boy was no big deal. Now everyone wants to make something of it. "Is he your boyfriend?" "Are you two in love?" "Oooooooh." Hang out with a boy, and some kids just don't want to leave you alone.

Point number 1

Having a guy friend is a great thing for a girl. It gives you a chance to relax with a boy, to talk with him and get to know him without the feelings and responsibilities that come with a romance. It means you see boys as regular people, not creatures from the Black Lagoon. It means you'll have fewer misconceptions about boys when you get into a romantic relationship with one. The last thing you want to do is throw away a friendship like this just because some bean-brain's decided to tease you about it.

So here's the plan: Teasers want you to be embarrassed. **Don't cooperate.** Look them in the eye and say, "No, we're just friends." Do the same thing the next 85 times they ask the question. Eventually they'll get bored and go on to something else.

Five years from now, girl-boy friendships will be common. Act like you know what you're doing—because you do—and, in the end, other kids will get the picture.

Point number 2

That said, it's also true that some girls aren't quite sure what to make of their feelings for their boy buds. If other kids are pairing up, you may look at your (boy) friend and think, *Why not?*

Pairing up with a friend sometimes works out great. Friendship is at the bottom of all good relationships. You two might find you can communicate a whole lot better than two kids who weren't friends before. You know something about each other's likes and dislikes. You're relaxed. You know how to have fun together.

At the same time, being "boyfriend and girlfriend" in the world of who-likes-who is often a lot more complicated than being friends.

Other people ~~may~~ will try harder to tell you what to do:

And what you expect from each other may change:

The upshot is that **sometimes** a girl who makes her friend her boyfriend may realize she preferred things the way they were before.

It may be fairly easy for two friends to go back to being the way they were.

WARNING

But it may not.

If his feelings were hurt, he may no longer trust you the way he did before you tried out the boyfriend-girlfriend roles. The old friendship may take a long time to put back together—if it gets put back together at all.

So if you're thinking about making a bud into a boyfriend, think twice. If it feels right (only you can tell), go ahead, but talk it over with him first. Make a pact together about how you'll treat each other if things don't work out. Then stick to it.

boys vs. buds

A girl may find herself torn between a boy and her friends.

Defending your choice

I really like this guy, but my friends think he's a nerd. I can't lie and say that now I think he's a nerd. They already know I like him.

Boy troubled

It's not easy to stand up to friends who belittle the boy you like. You may worry about their friendship and doubt your own judgment. It may seem safer to put your heart in the fridge—to like the boys your friends like and dismiss the boys your friends dismiss. But what does that get you?

- Friends you can't be honest with
- Boys you don't like much
- The feeling of defeat that comes from throwing away your own convictions

The best thing to do if your friends say this boy's a nerd? Look them in the eye and tell them why they're wrong.

Him vs. Her

My boyfriend and best friend hate each other. Every day it's always, "Why are you her friend?" from my boyfriend and "Why don't you break up with him?" from my best friend. I'm always trapped. They are nasty to each other, and I'm sick of it.

Caught in the Middle

Yeesh. What an unpleasant situation. Both your friend and your boyfriend are out of line. Tell them so. Tell this boy: "I know you don't like my friend, but I do. Please stop nagging me about her." Say the same thing to your friend. You can't ask them to be friends; but you can ask them to stop bugging you. Demand a truce.

Bad guy

My friend has a boyfriend who's no good. He is mean to little kids, and he wrote her a bad note about her old boyfriend. My friend doesn't realize he's doing this, and if I tell her, she might be mad at me.

Texas girl

She's going to have to figure this out for herself. You can help her do that by being honest about your own opinions and giving her information she should have. (Just be sure of your facts.) But if you nag, she'll wall you out. Say what you have to say, then stay out of it, knowing you've done what you could.

Fear of friends

A boy I like just asked me out, and I said yes. Now I'm afraid my friends won't like me or will think I'm a loser because they don't like him. Should I break up or lose my friends?

Puzzled in Providence

Whoa. Sometimes a girl looks at a boy with her own eyes and sees one thing. Then she looks at him through her friends' eyes and sees another. But you're worried about your friends' opinion before they've even had a chance to offer it. You're worrying too much, too soon.

The question you need to ask yourself isn't "Should I break up or lose my friends?" It's "Why did I say yes to this boy to begin with?"

Did you say yes even though you don't like him much, because saying no was harder? If so, you should talk to him kindly and privately and say you made a mistake. If, however, you said yes because you wanted to, because you like him, then tell your friends what you've done. Give them—and this boy—a chance.

Judging a guy

I like this guy. The problem is, all my friends say I shouldn't. They think he is mean and inconsiderate, but he's always been extremely kind to me.

To Trust friends (or not!)

He's kind to you—so far, so good. But if your friends say he's mean, give him a second look. Watch how he treats other people. What's he like with the popular kids? With your friends?

With the least popular kids? What's he like with adults and younger kids? When a boy and girl first like each other, both are on their best behavior. But best behavior isn't regular behavior. And it's his regular behavior that's going to tell you who this boy really is. It takes time to get to know someone, which is one big reason to go slow with any boy.

Trouble with his buds

There's this boy in my class, and we started going out. He really liked me, but one day he broke up with me because one of his friends doesn't like me. It really hurt because he broke up with me with a rude note telling me how much he hates me.

Mary

You've learned the hard way what to expect from people who let their friends do their thinking for them. This guy's made you a sadder, wiser girl—but the sadness won't last. The wisdom will.

boys online

So you like to write e-mails, eh? O.K. So do we all. Chat rooms and instant messages can be fun, too. But keep these things in mind when you're on the Net:

- **E-mails aren't private.** They feel that way because you write them alone in your room, but they can end up every bit as public as a note you wrote in school and lost in the lunchroom. Any e-mail can be printed or forwarded to dozens of people with a click of the mouse. Consider, too, that your message may exist on a hard drive in (at least) two homes, and anyone who boots up the machines may be able to read it.

- **Think before you type.** People tend to say things using a keyboard that they would never say face to face. The part of their brain that whispers, "Maybe I shouldn't get carried away here" is asleep. Before you pour out your heart (or your temper) onscreen, ask yourself: "Would I say this if I were writing a letter or talking to this person? Am I going to be sorry I said this tomorrow?" Protect yourself. Use your manners, too. There are real human beings on the other end.

- **Be honest.** You don't want other people to lie to you about who they are online. Don't lie to them. It's dishonest and can be hurtful.

- **Keep your guard up.** When you're talking to someone online, you can have no idea who that person really is. "Billy" may be a sixth-grader in New York, as he says he is; but he may be a full-grown man in Nevada, too. There is simply no way to be sure.

You know the rest: **Never** identify yourself to somebody online—not by name, not by town or school or address. Be very wary of profiles: the less you say about yourself the better. If you're in a chatroom and someone starts saying things that make you uncomfortable, log off instantly and report it to the chat-room supervisor. Keep your parents up to date on all online contacts—the people you chat with regularly and the people who send you messages. And, needless to say, never agree to meet anybody you've met online.

But you **can't be sure—**that's the whole point. There are people out there who are very clever at manipulating other people. You simply **cannot take the chance.**

Too, if you've come to depend so very much on your relationship with a person who exists only as type on a screen, it's time to ask yourself if you shouldn't turn off the machine and see who you can meet in the world of flesh and blood. Bag the virtual relationship. Try one where you can hear the guy laugh and tap him on the shoulder when you need him.

parties & dances

Gak! It's your first boy-girl party. So many questions!

Q: I don't have a boyfriend. I'll feel nervous. Should I just stay home?

A: You don't need a boyfriend to go to a boy-girl party. Go ahead and go. Chances are good that there will be plenty of people there just like you to hang out with.

Q: I've heard that sometimes people play a kissing game. What if I don't want to play?

A: Say, "No, thanks, I'll pass." Make yourself the DJ, and go pick out the next batch of CDs.

Q: My parents won't let me go. What do I do?

A: You could ask your parents to talk to the parents of the person having the party. If they knew more about what's planned for the event and what sort of adult supervision there will be, they might change their minds.

Q: Can I ask a boy to dance?

A: Absolutely. A lot of boys are itching to dance but don't have the nerve to make the first move. If you do, go for it.

Q: I don't know how to dance. What if somebody asks me?

A: Say, "I'm not a good dancer." He'll probably say something like "I'm not, either," or "That's O.K." Then you can go out and give it a try—which is, after all, the way to learn. If you are just too uncomfortable to do that? Tell the boy, "Thanks for asking, but I'm not a good dancer. I'm going to sit out the dancing."

Q: What do I wear?

A: Call your friends and see what they're wearing. Then go to your closet and pick something that makes you feel good.

Q: That was fun. Now I'd kind of like to have a boy-girl party myself.

A: Talk to your parents. Where's it going to be? What activities will you offer? Think it all out before you proceed.

Invite your real friends—not people you think would look good at a boy-girl party. You'll want some food and drink, but it doesn't have to be fancy. (Everybody likes popcorn, right?) Ask your friends to bring their favorite CDs. Most important, make sure there's something for people to do besides dance. If you have a table game—pool, Ping-Pong, Foosball—you're home free. Darts are good, too (if they're the safe variety). You could also set out board games or cards, or try goofier stuff, like Mad Libs, the limbo, or charades.

popularity

Of course, it isn't just your friends you need to live with. There's all those other kids out there—especially . . .

able to leap the social ladder in a single bound,

more glamorous than a bike with RockShox,

faster than a speeding goal kick . . .

... the popular kids.

If you're "popular," it feels pretty good (although not as good as the kids who aren't popular imagine it does). If you aren't "popular," you probably have mixed feelings about the kids who are.

If you care about popularity, it can **warp** the way you see yourself. It can give you warped ideas about boys as well.

Some warped and dumb ideas:

Dumb idea = Having a boyfriend makes you more popular.

Truth = *The popular girls have boyfriends, so if I have a boyfriend, I'll be popular, too*—that's the logic. But it doesn't work, anymore than copycatting ever works. You're still going to be you—only you'll be squinched up inside from trying to be somebody else.

Dumb idea = If you get friendly with a boy, it had better be a boy who's at least as popular as you are. Otherwise, your own popularity will go down.

Truth = The only kind of popularity that's worth anything comes from respect.

A good way to gain the respect of other kids is to act with independence and confidence.

A good way to lose it is to weigh people's popularity before you decide who you want to hang out with.

Dumb idea = The great boys are the popular boys.

Truth = Great boys come in all kinds of flavors—kind, funny, considerate, smart, sweet, interesting, brave, talented, amazing . . . But "popular" isn't one of them.

Lots of wonderful guys are popular. But a jerk can be popular, too. And a jerk is a jerk.

teasing & harassment

Every day at school, boys make fun of me about my body. I go to sit down off to the side, but they still go on, even though they know it hurts and embarrasses me.

Megan

Teasing goes on in schools from Day One. Some teasing is a sign of affection. Some is pure meanness. When kids begin entering puberty, lots of teasing takes a new, more sexual turn.

Flirting pretty much always involves teasing. Usually it's light and fun, and everybody walks away feeling good.

But some kids don't know where to stop. Their conversations are full of sexual jokes and comments about bodies. For them, boldness is a game. Boys, in particular, want to be daring. They may like getting reactions from other people and may push the edges of what's considered private and polite. It's partly about impressing their friends. It's partly about impressing you.

For instance, a boy might make a comment about another girl's body in front of you. Or he might make a joke about your kissing him, or more. He wants you to blush and laugh and be impressed with how brash he is. Don't be afraid to draw a line at talk that makes you uncomfortable:

If the boy is worth your time—and your friendship—he'll stop.

And if he doesn't? In a lot of cases, the boy is just immature and out of control. You can walk off, and it's easy enough to go through life without having much to do with him. Now and then, however, a boy keeps it up to the point that it becomes a real problem for a girl.

In fact, a lot of so-called friendly teasing qualifies as harassment. **It's against the law.**

In the worst cases, sexual talk and teasing are used to out-and-out humiliate a girl. A girl may get teased for having big breasts or small ones. A boy or group of boys may corner a girl and make sexual remarks with the sole purpose of upsetting her. Occasionally a boy or group of boys will touch a girl in a sexual way without her permission.

How you should handle harassment if it happens to you depends on how serious it is.

Plan A

If the boy doesn't scare you, and the harassment isn't too frequent, you'll want to start by trying to handle it yourself. How? By standing up to him.

- Bullies like **easy victims.** Don't be one. Don't duck your head and walk on by when a boy makes a sexual comment. He *wants* you to be embarrassed. Look him in the eye. Say his name and tell him what you think of what he's said. "John Smith, that's an insulting remark." He may laugh and make some comeback to save face in front of his friends, but he may also hear you.

- Let a boy know you've got **limits.** "I'm going to let it go this time, because your brain's as big as a flea, and I feel sorry for you. But next time I'm turning you in." And if there is a next time, do it.

Plan B

If none of this works, or if the teasing is constant and aggressive, and what you're hearing is vile and scary, then you need to get help right away.

- **Parents** can be a big, big help in situations like this. If you tell them what's going on, they can take your case to other adults who can shut this boy down.

- Talk to **adults at school**—your teacher, the school counselor, and the principal. If they know what's happening, they can tell this boy just how serious the consequences for harassment can be—and *will* be for *him* if he doesn't back off.

- Your parents or someone from the school will have to talk to **this boy's parents.** He needs to hear it from all sides: his abuse of you has got to stop.

- If nobody seems able or willing to control this boy, ask your parents to put your complaint **in writing** to the school system. Use the words "sexual harassment." The people who run your school have a responsibility to make it a place all kids can go and learn. You've got every right to hold them to it.

Of course, you may be reading all this thinking:

Yes, it's very hard. But you've really got no choice. If you don't tell, the bullies have won. They're walking the halls full of themselves, and you're scared to go to school. You're taking the shame they should feel for tormenting you and carrying it around yourself.

Tell. Get help. Get your life back.

Put the shame where it belongs—on them.

peer pressure

Who's running your life? Circle your answer.

1. You tell your friends that you really like a certain guy. They say, "What? That geek?" You say:

a.

b.

c.

2. Your friend says, "Jamil likes you. I'll go tell him you like him back. Then you two will be going together." You feel like somebody stepped on your stomach. You say:

a.

b.

c.

3. Four boys showed up at the party, and here you are playing Truth or Dare. Sarah demands that you go in the back room with Will and kiss. Will's willing. You're not. You say:

a.

b.

c.

4 → Maureen is the most popular girl in the school. She appears at your locker one day and says, "Why do you spend so much time with Hal? I could fix you up with Eddie." You say:

5 → You and your buddy George are having a great time, like always, when Jaimie and her gang appear. She says, "Now we know who your boyfriend is!" You say:

answers

Chipper skipper
If you answered mostly **a**'s, you sail your own ship. You love your friends, but that doesn't mean you're going to let them do your thinking for you. If you get involved with a boy, it's going to be because you like him yourself—not because somebody else is pulling the strings.

Wishy washy
If you answered mostly **b**'s, you know what you want but are too cowed by your friends to say so. Try being up front. You may be surprised at how well it works—and pleased with how you feel about yourself afterward.

Puppy dog
If you answered mostly **c**'s, you're letting your friends lead you around. You might as well be on a leash. You've got your own brain and your own beliefs. Act on them! You're going to find yourself in one ratty situation after the next until the day you say, "No, I'm deciding this myself."

Going Together

twosomes

So you and your friends have started to hang out now and then with a certain group of boys. Maybe you do stuff together at recess or meet at Micky D's after school. Some of you are having crushes. Some of you aren't. Either way, it's exciting for you to be with a bunch of boys. Yet being with your friends makes you feel happy and secure, too.

Eventually, some of the group will probably decide to try going together. Should you? It may feel like a little step, but it will make a difference in how you relate to the boy you like. So don't roll into it on automatic. Give it some thought. See what your parents have to say. And make sure that if you're going to have an "official" boyfriend, it's for a good reason.

POP QUIZ

why pair off?

And just what *is* a good reason for going with a guy? Circle your answers.

1. Your best friend says you should.
2. He's nice, brainy, cute, and fun to be with.
3. He's popular.
4. All your other friends have boyfriends, and you don't want to be left out.
5. All the popular kids have boyfriends.
6. You want to make another guy jealous.
7. You're afraid to say no when he asks.
8. You've got a crush on his best friend.
9. You feel good when you're around him.
10. He's the only guy who's asked, and you want to go with *somebody.*
11. You don't want people to think you're too chicken.
12. It's what girls your age do.

answers

Good reasons: 2 and 9. **Bad reasons:** All the rest.

Explanation: Do you really need one?

things to do when you go out

A lot of kids "go together" without ever actually going anywhere together at all. But that doesn't have to be the case. There are lots of things you and your boyfriend (and your friends and his) can do to have fun.

Go **Rollerblading.** Teach him how to stop.

Summertime? Lovely. Your group can meet his at the **pool.**

How about a round of **mini golf?** Show no mercy.

Get your friends together and go **bowling.** Bumpers? Don't even think about it.

A **walk** around the neighborhood in springtime isn't half bad.

Your brother's on the hockey team at the high school? Cool. Invite your guy to go to a **game** with your family.

Hungry? Stop at the bagel shop. See what weird stuff they're putting in the cream cheese today.

It's **open gym.** Don't just stand there. Get a boy-girl volleyball game together.

Sledding. It's not just for first-graders. Maybe Mom can make hot cocoa for half the hill afterward.

You and your friends wanted to see that **movie,** right? So ask him and his friends to meet you there.

O.K., O.K.—there's always the **mall.** Just be aware that he may not like to shop in the same stores for the same things that you do.

Sit on the steps and **talk.**

Having tickets to the water park is great, but sometimes just hanging out with someone you like is even better. It's the **spirit** you bring to what you do that matters.

touching

When you were a baby, you enjoyed getting cuddled and stroked. When you got a little older, you enjoyed sitting in your parents' laps and feeling their arms around you. Even now, you may like having a friend comb your hair and braid it, or like the feeling you get walking down the street with your arm flung over a friend's shoulders. There's something wonderful about touching a person you care for. There may come a time you will enjoy a physical relationship with a boy, too.

Boy-girl touching usually begins with holding hands, a first dance, or a first kiss.

Sometimes a first kiss is magical and wonderful. Sometimes it's . . .

funny disappointing sad embarrassing goofy sweet

Some people totally forget their first kiss when they're older. Others remember everything about it:

I was in first grade, delivering a May basket. This boy popped out of the house and told me the tradition was that if you gave somebody a May basket, he got to kiss you. I didn't know any better, so I let him do it. I didn't have another kiss till I was a senior in high school.

Susie

I was 12. I'd been going out with my twin brother's best friend since fourth grade, but we hadn't gone anywhere, let alone kissed. My brother thought this was awful. One day when the three of us were playing football, he said the loser had to kiss the winner. Then he made sure I lost. So I kissed Mark (it was quick!), and we continued to play. My brother was so proud of himself.

Jeannine

I was in fourth grade. We'd just learned the rules for spin the bottle. Naturally, the boys controlled the bottle. The first time I kissed Jane, I hardly knew what to do. She turned her head so I barely grazed her cheek, and in the process I sneezed. The best was when Jane kissed me. Her lips scarcely touched the corner of my mouth, but her hair brushed my face, I smelled her sweetness, and her eyes closed.

Tom

I was 14. The boy I had a crush on took me to his mother's wedding. After the ceremony, we took a walk and he kissed me behind a tree. I floated all the way home.

Harriet

I was 14. I was watching a movie outdoors at the day camp where I worked, and I was kissed by this boy I'd had a crush on for months. I was so euphoric I didn't eat for three days, and my mom took me to the doctor.

Deb

My first kiss was a first miss. Kent asked, "Well, can I?" I said, "I guess so." He put the arm that wasn't carrying the football around my waist. I closed my eyes and felt his forehead graze my ear. Then came a sort of muffled snort. He seemed to be smelling my hair. "Well, I guess, bye," he muttered, then sprinted away. There was clearly something unkissable about me. I wept. An entire miserable week later, Kent confessed that he had truly intended to kiss me but had, in fact, missed.

Judy

The summer before seventh grade, my cousin double-dog-dared me to kiss Aaron behind the pool. She thought that because we shared the same first name, we were destined to be together. She was wrong. The kiss lasted two seconds—one second longer than the relationship. She was promptly fired from matchmaking duties.

Erin

Kissing basics

1. It's not a race. Just because your friend kissed a boy last week doesn't mean you have to run out and kiss a boy tomorrow. You've got years ahead of you. A first romance is fun if you're with a boy you really like, and it's not much fun at all if you're not.

2. Make it private. A kiss is meant for two people, not 20. Keep it that way.

3. If you kiss a boy, it should be because you want to—not because he talked you into it. That goes for all other touching, too. If a boy says:

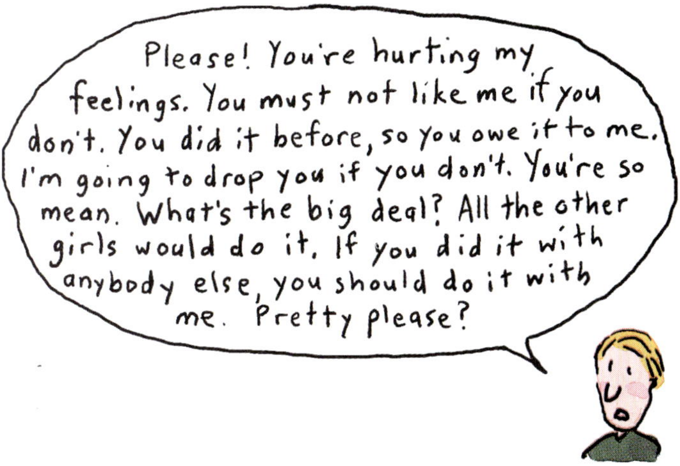

Your answer should be:

trouble-starters

There are a hundred tried-and-true ways to stir up trouble in a relationship. What are the things that bug people the most?

Boys say:

When girls pressure you to do everything. You're supposed to be the one who calls them. They get mad if you don't. You're supposed to ask them out, to pay for everything. They just sit there.

Joey, age 13

If a girl talks nonstop about nothing.

Ian, age 12

When girls call too much. If they have to call, they should call once and get the whole story, not call five times. And the most annoying thing is that sparkly eye shadow. Makeup should be worn in moderation.

Andrew, age 13

When a girl talks a lot, takes a long time in stores, complains, and does the "like-like-like" thing.

Aaron, age 13

Being all perky is annoying. So is never giving an honest point of view.

Connor, age 12

When a girl acts all depressed, like "Oh, you hate me," for no reason.

Ike, age 13

Girls say:

When boys aren't themselves. They try to be cool and wind up acting really stupid.

Jenny, age 13

If a boy flirts with other girls and talks about other girls to you.

Meredith, age 13

If boys talk about themselves too much and act full of themselves.

Jessie, age 13

When they ignore you if they're with their friends.

Luba, age 13

Some boys pressure girls to do things they don't want to do.

Laura, age 13

They worry about their hair and clothes and what they look like.

Molly, age 12

They don't talk to you and almost avoid you.

Megan, age 12

solving problems

You're mad. Or he's mad. Or you're both mad. Does that mean it's over? Not necessarily.

What's the problem? Think before you blow. Decide what's truly bugging you. Is it really what your boyfriend did this morning or what he said to you last week? Think about it. Talk about it with your big sister or your mom or dad. Get it clear in your head. You can't fix a problem until you know for sure what it is.

Pick a good time. Some conversations are doomed because of when and where they take place. It's just not a good idea to launch into a topic that upsets both of you 30 seconds before the bell rings. You need privacy. You need time.

Talk about it. Tell him what you're unhappy about. Tell him what you want to have happen.

Listen. Give him time to give his view, too. If he seems reluctant to talk, and impatient to get the conversation over with, say, "I know this is hard to talk about, but I think it's important that we figure this out."

Don't be afraid to disagree. You know how to compromise and negotiate, and that's great. But it's just as important to say what you think. So screw up your courage and do so. And don't get offended by a boy who does the same thing. Boys may express themselves more bluntly when they disagree.

Expect some outbursts. Chances are, you'll get excited and he'll get excited, and both of you will say some things you don't mean. When you hear yourself going overboard, admit it: "I'm exaggerating, but that's how it felt!"

Make a plan. Try to walk away with some kind of plan to make things better. "O.K. I'll go, and you'll call me later." Even if you're both still riled up inside, it's going to feel good to have agreed on something.

problem boyfriends

Don't let a problem boyfriend walk all over you.

Phone shy

My boyfriend never calls me, so I have to call him. One time, I called him and asked him why, and he said, "I'm busy and I'm never free to talk." All I said was, "Well try, at least." And he said he had to go. What does this mean? Should I dump him?

Hannah

Don't expect to have the same kind of conversations with your boyfriend that you have with your friends. Talking is the glue that holds together girls' friendships. For a boy, friendship is more about doing things together. Put two girls in a room and they may well sit on the rug and talk. Put two boys in a room and they're more likely to start shooting hoops with a Nerf ball. Boys just aren't as comfortable talking about their feelings as girls. And many aren't going to be ready to have long talks on the phone.

What's your relationship like with this boy otherwise? Do you have fun when you see each other at school? Does he seem to enjoy your company when you're together other times? If so, don't make a big issue over the phone.

Neglectful

I think my boyfriend doesn't like me very much. He pays more attention to other girls than me.

Amber

First, a quick double-check: ask yourself if you're sure about this. You don't want to be overpossessive—a girl who turns green around the gills anytime her boyfriend talks to another girl.

If you *are* sure—if he flirts with other girls and ignores you—then you should talk to him about it. If you don't hear something like "I'm sorry. I still like you best," you need to pull the plug on this guy.

You deserve good treatment. Don't settle for anything less.

Broken promises

I have a boyfriend who keeps promising to do things but then doesn't. But he also does nice things for me. Should I dump him or not?

Unsure

It could be that this boy gets carried away and makes promises he can't keep. If he's full of good feelings for you and a little scatterbrained, maybe you can live with it.

If he's insincere, that's another kettle of fish. Do you think he knows at the moment he makes the promises that he's not going to follow up? If so, he's being manipulative, and that's not good. No boy's perfect. But a guy who can't give you the truth isn't giving you respect, either.

problem girlfriends

What's the smart move for a girl who cares about a relationship? Check your answers.

1 → You're coming out of class when you see your boyfriend talking to three girls. You march up and say, "Why are you flirting with other girls?"

☐ Good move ☐ Bad move

2 → "What are you doing this afternoon?" you ask your boyfriend. "What are you doing tonight? What are you doing tomorrow? What are you doing this weekend?"

☐ Good move ☐ Bad move

3 → You and your boyfriend were planning to meet at the mall today. He calls and says, "Sorry, I forgot I have soccer practice." You say, "No problem," and go do something else.

☐ Good move ☐ Bad move

4 → You're talking to the most popular boy in the school. Your boyfriend walks by. You ignore him.

☐ Good move ☐ Bad move

5 → You and your boyfriend and your friends are walking to school. You talk only to your friends. Why bother with him? He's just a boy.

☐ Good move ☐ Bad move

6 → Your boyfriend really ticked you off this morning. To punish him, you threaten to dump him.

☐ Good move ☐ Bad move

answers

1. **Bad move.**
Unless your boyfriend lives in a cave 50 miles from town, he's going to have friendships with other people, boys and girls both. Get used to it. If you can't, your jealousy is going to make life miserable for you both. A good relationship runs on trust and confidence. If you've lost those things, there's nothing left.

2. **Bad move.**
Make your boyfriend report to you all the time about where he goes and whom he sees, and he's going to feel like a dog on a two-inch leash. First chance he gets, he'll bolt. And who can blame him?

3. **Good move.**
Being relaxed is always a good move. Don't take everything personally.

4. **Bad move.**
Come on! How two-faced is that? This isn't some game where you toss a person onto the discard pile the minute you see a chance to pick up a higher card.

5. **Bad move.**
Consider how you'd feel if your boyfriend ignored you in front of his friends. Awkward, left out, hurt . . . resentful, maybe. Including everybody in the conversation is basic courtesy.

6. **Bad move.**
If you've got a problem, deal with it. Making threats is fighting dirty.

time to break up?

POP QUIZ

There are times a girl should walk away from a boy and times she shouldn't. What's your answer?

1. You go to the movies with your boyfriend. He sees his friends. He leaves you and sits with them. Stuff like this has been going on for weeks.

   ☐ Hold on ☐ Break up

2. You can't get your boyfriend on the phone. His mother says he's with his friends. But you can't be sure.

   ☐ Hold on ☐ Break up

3. You decided to go with this boy because you were curious to see what it would be like. Now you know. It's weird and awkward and complicated, and you wish you were free to be yourself again.

   ☐ Hold on ☐ Break up

4. Your boyfriend is nice and all, but the truth is you've started liking somebody else. You don't want to hurt his feelings.

   ☐ Hold on ☐ Break up

5. He's the only boy you've ever liked, but he's been soooo frustrating this week.

   ☐ Hold on ☐ Break up

answers

Hold on

The best answer to **2** and **5** is **hold on.** Don't throw out a good relationship for a small or temporary problem. Fix the problem.

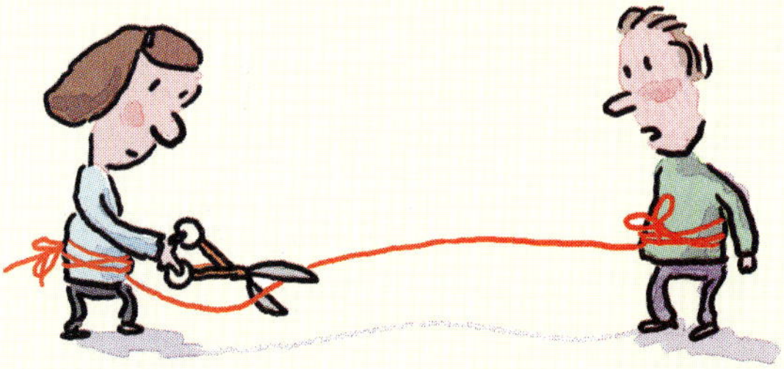

Break up

The best answer to **1, 3,** and **4** is **break up.**

There's no reason to stay with a boy who treats you badly. Now or ever. And there's no point in staying with a boy if your heart isn't in it, either.

Ending a relationship isn't easy. But it's a whole lot easier than getting up every day knowing that you're in a relationship that isn't right.

how to break up

You know it's got to be done. But if you're like most girls, you're feeling a little **chicken.**

Could you go to Antarctica and call him from there? Or what if you pretended you have amnesia and don't know who he is? Maybe if your friends all said you died . . . Is there *nothing* that will save you from having to face him and say what you've got to say?

No. As the saying goes, you can run but you **can't hide.** A lot of nice girls do cruel things to boys at moments like these because they feel awkward about delivering bad news. Don't be one of them. Do it right.

Keep it **private.** Telling him at school may be convenient, but it's cruel. And making your girlfriend your messenger is the pits. This is between you and this boy. Keep his friends and your friends out of it.

You can **talk to him.** Or you can **write a note** and talk to him later. Either way, you *do* have to talk to him. Freezing him out because you don't know what to say is *not* an option.

When you break the news, say something more than "I don't want to go out with you anymore." Give him a **reason.** Be honest. But don't be mean.

Put some thought into **your words,** too. "I think we'd both have more fun if we saw other people" is better than "You really bug me." "We don't get along that well" is better than "You're a jerk." "I liked it better when we were just friends" is better than "I'm sorry I ever said I'd go out with you."

Will any of these lines make him smile and say, "That's O.K."? Not likely. He'll still be hurt and may well be angry—but not nearly so hurt and angry as he'd be if you did it in a way that showed you were thinking only of yourself. (And after a day or two, he may be as relieved as you are to be out of the relationship.)

getting dumped

A few weeks ago, my boyfriend and I broke up. The reason I am taking it so hard is that I really thought he was "The One."

Lonely in Texas

Dumped. What a word. It sounds so much like "garbage," which may pretty much be the way you feel the first time it happens to you.

Sometimes you can see a dump coming. Inside, you know things aren't right. Before you do something about it, he does, and *wham.* You've been dumped. A blow to the pride? Sure. Yet, when the dust settles, you find your feelings are fine.

Of course, there are also times when the dump comes as a total surprise from a boy you still really like. What do you do then? The same kinds of things you've always done when bad things happen.

Talk to your mom or dad, your sister or brother, your Aunt Mavis or your cousin Kath. Pick a good shoulder to cry on and let go.

When you're out of tears, go for a swim, or break out the skates or the bike or the hockey stick. Make it a point to **do something physical every day.**

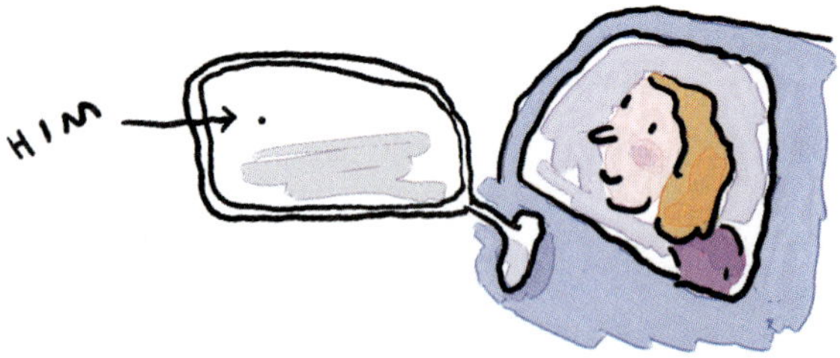

Call friends. Make plans. Don't sit around feeling sorry for yourself. **Keep life moving.** Pretty soon this boy will be a speck in your rearview mirror.

Taking Care of You

how are you doing?

Has the world of who-likes-who changed the way you think?

1 → Ever since school started, you've felt bad because no boy has any interest in you. You've started making lists in your head of all the things that are wrong with you.

☐ That's me. ☐ That's not me.

2 → Darla told Dan that you liked Dennis, and Dan told Doug. Doug likes you, so he got discouraged and told Deb. Deb likes Dennis, so she got mad and told lies about you and Dan to Diane, who repeated them at the dance to Dennis, who told Darla he didn't like you anymore. Darla told you in the donut shop. You got mad and wrote a note to Dennis. You had Denise give it to Dane to give to Dennis, only Dane had a dentist appointment and left early. So you called Dennis that night. Then you called Darla and Deb and Dan and Doug and Denise and Dane. Turns out that Denise was mad at Deb . . .

Then you walk into
Spanish and realize—
Today's the test!

☐ That's me. ☐ That's not me.

3 You are crazy, crazy about one particular boy. If you had to choose between him and your best friend, you'd go with the boy.

☐ That's me. ☐ That's not me.

4 No boy will ever like you. You're too ugly. Pretty girls fill you with feelings you don't even want to discuss.

☐ That's me. ☐ That's not me.

5 Jack wants you to come to the 7-Eleven. "So what if your parents say you can't. Don't be a wuss." You go. You'd do anything to make him like you.

☐ That's me. ☐ That's not me.

answers

If you said "that's me," here's what you need to know:

1. Having a lot of boys calling you every night doesn't make you a better person. Having no boys calling doesn't make you a worse one. Judge yourself on **character,** not boyfriends.

2. Trying to talk to an entire school is like fighting a monster with seven heads. Keep it **simple.** If you have a problem with a person, go to that person. Don't use messengers. Don't be one.

3. Look around. How many boy-girl couples do you see that last more than a month? More than a year? The fact is, boys come and go in a girl's life. Good friends don't. Friendships are **precious.** Don't forget it. Don't throw one away over a boy.

4 → A lot of normal-looking girls get so anxious about pleasing boys that they decide they're "ugly." Yes, beauty counts with boys. And, yes, not all girls have it. But worrying about your looks is a big, wide road to nowhere. Your face is your face. You can compare yourself with the prettiest of girls and fill up with jealousy and shame. Or you can forget the mirror and get going with your **life.**

Put some energy into being fit and healthy. Keep yourself clean. Have fun with your clothes and your style. Have some faith in yourself.

As anyone over 18 can tell you, the "pretty girls" in sixth grade are not always the "pretty girls" in college. People change. And what boys and girls look for in one another changes, too. A lot of qualities that get overlooked in sixth grade—cleverness, creativity, conviction—get more important later on. There's going to be someone for you. He may not show up this year. He may not show up the year after that. But he'll be there. And he'll be in love with **you,** not with your face.

5 → Don't get stupid. Never give up your own point of view. Always **stand up** for what you deserve. A girl who'll do anything to please a boy wins nobody's respect. Not the boy's. Not her own.

happy ever after?

You've had ups and downs with friends over the years. You're going to have some ups and downs with boys, too. It's all part of **growing up.**

What you want to remember along the way is this: You've got so much to find out about yourself—interests to explore, talents to develop. Sure, relationships will be important to you. But good relationships

truly **truly** **truly**

depend on both people feeling good about themselves. Your happiness doesn't depend on hitching yourself to the boy of your dreams. It depends on finding out what you love to do in the world, and doing it. Put your heart in you—in your hopes for the future, your plans for what you can do and create, experience and enjoy. It'll make you strong and confident and ready for anything, including **love.**